Marcus Aurelius

Roman Emperor and Stoic
Philosopher

Table of Contents

Introduction

Marcus Aurelius was the Emperor of the Roman Empire from 161 to 180 A.D. He is considered to be the last of the Five Good Emperors, the first four of whom were Nerva, Trajan, Hadrian, and Antoninus Pius. Marcus is also best remembered as the author of Meditations, a highly revered work on the philosophy of Stoicism.

Interestingly, none of these five people were connected through the same bloodline. They were all from different families and took on the mantle of the Roman Emperor as ordained by their predecessors, who envisioned their chosen successors to be fit enough for the majestic role.

- The reasons why these five were known as Five Good Emperors are many. Some of the most notable greatness of the Roman Empire happened during these people's reigns.

- This period witnessed a considerable expansion of the Roman Empire's frontier, ranging from northern Britain to Dacia in central Europe, Arabia, and Mesopotamia.

- The defense systems were perfected, making it difficult for invaders to enter and take control of any Roman territories.

- A fairly uniform provincial system was in place right across the Empire, ensuring the smooth governance and functioning of public offices and related machinery.

- All the people across the Empire were slowly but surely Romanized in terms of culture and language.

All the above great things occurred during the rule of Marcus Aurelius too. Yet, his life was never free from strife and struggle. The best part was he bore it like a true Stoic.

Plato, one of the Big Three (the other two being Socrates, Plato's teacher, and Aristotle, Plato's student), is believed to have coined the term "philosopher-king" in his work titled Republic. According to Plato, the kind of ruler who can provide the best form of governance would be one who was a philosopher too because a philosopher-king seeks power, not for his personal benefit but using it for the good of his people.

Marcus Aurelius is believed to be a perfect embodiment of Plato's concept of "philosopher-king." He believed in being responsible for others. This ideal is evident from an important quote from his book Meditations, which goes something like this: "Human beings exist for one another, and therefore, we should teach the less learned, help the less privileged, and bear with everyone's weaknesses."

Marcus Aurelius was introduced to philosophy at a very young age, and his daily philosophical musings, which are collected together in Meditations, were written in his 50s while on military campaigns. This reflects the fact that this Roman Emperor a deep Stoical view right through his life.

Marcus' entire reign is defined by Stoicism and its tenets. In fact, a historian, Cassius Dio, who lived during 155 - 235 A.D. called Marcus as 'the philosopher.' Cassius Dio is believed to be the author (or one of the many authors) of Historia Augustus, a collection of the histories of Roman Emperors.

Marcus lived like a Stoic in his personal and public lives, including during his youth when he held important public positions and as the Emperor of the Roman Empire. True to Stoic principles, Marcus Aurelius placed the needs of others above his own needs and desires.

And yet, ironically, Marcus' reign is characterized by constant wars, diseases, and persecution by leaders and followers of the new religion, Christianity. In fact, some historians tend to put his reign as the beginning of the end of the Roman Empire.

Despite all these pressures, Marcus Aurelius did not waver from his responsibility of being a just and good emperor. He went on multiple military campaigns and used both defensive and offensive attacks to keep peace in his Empire and to expand its territories, respectively. He managed to rule his Empire efficiently and bring about important policy changes for the welfare of the less privileged citizens. Immediately after his death (due to natural causes) in 180 A.D., he was revered as one of the best Roman Emperors.

Sadly for Marcus, his choice of his successor was not taken very well by the Romans. His son,

Commodus, whom Marcus anointed as his successor before he died in 180 A.D., turned out quite badly as a ruler. In fact, historians easily label him as one of the worst rulers the Roman Empire had ever put up with. The fact that Commodus was continually compared to his illustrious father made it worse for him.

No matter what his son turned out to be, there is no denying the fact that Marcus Aurelius was one of the best rulers in the history of mankind, and his lessons continue to impact and inspire us to this day, nearly 2000 years after his passing! That is truly historic.

Chapter One:

Childhood and Youth

M arcus Aurelius was born on April 26, 121 A.D. in Spain into a politically prominent and wealthy noble family in Rome. His paternal grandfather was the prefect and consul of Rome for the second time at the time of Marcus' birth. Marcus' original name given by his parents was Marcus Annius Verus.

He had an excellent education and was known to have been a master at Greek and Latin. Even as a student, Marcus' interest in philosophy, especially Stoicism, was clearly evident. Stoicism was an established school of philosophy that promoted the ideas of self-restraint, fate, and the use of logic and reason to lead a happy, contented life.

Marcus' family was highly connected with the people in power in the Roman Empire. His aunt, or his father's sister, was married to Pius Antoninus too (more about him later). And his paternal grandfather's rise to become the perfect and consul of Rome was no mean feat.

Consuls in the Roman Empire were very powerful. As second in command after the Emperor, consuls presided over the Roman Senate and convened Senate meetings. They commanded the Roman Army. They had the power to execute decrees and were also ex-officio dignitaries representing the Roman Empire in foreign countries.

His mother, Domitia Luciall, also came from a wealthy, prominent family. Marcus' maternal grandmother was the heiress to one of the wealthiest and most influential families in Rome. Therefore, Marcus had his roots in one of the most revered Roman noble families that flourished both socially and politically under the patronage of the Flavian Emperors.

The Emperors of the Flavian Dynasty were known for their humble origins, piety, humility, and sobriety. They were popular among the Romans for the good works they did. They were also far more attuned to strong religious beliefs and morality than the preceding dynasty, the Julio-Claudian Dynasty, infamous for their extravagance, cynicism, and amoral attitude. The influence of Flavian character-istics was clearly evident in the growth and devel-opment of Marcus Aurelius' character, especially as the Roman Emperor.

Marcus' father died in 124 A.D., within just three years of his birth. He was, therefore, raised by nurses and governesses under the watchful eyes of his grandparents. Details about his young days are quite scarce, although most historians agree that he was a hard-working, committed pupil devouring Latin and Greek lessons with ease and elan. That he was taught both Latin and Greek reflects the inten-tions of his grandfathers to groom their grandchild for public life quite early.

The dedication and hard-working attitude of Marcus during his student days was noticed by Em-peror Hadrian, who was the imperial ruler of the Roman Empire during that time. As fate would have it, the earlier choice of Emperor Hadrian's successor had died, after which he had chosen Titus Aurelius Antoninus to succeed him under the title of Emper-or Pius Antoninus, who was the uncle of Marcus.

Emperor Hadrian, during his lifetime, also ensured that Emperor Pius Antoninus adopted

Marcus, ensuring that young Marcus would be the third in line to the throne of the Roman Empire after Emperor Hadrian. That is how impressed Hadrian was with Marcus.

So, at around 17 years of age, Marcus was adopted as the son of Antoninus, and Marcus Annius Verus' official name was changed to Caesar Marcus Aurelius Antoninus Augustus. His adopted father taught him politics, along with how to govern and administer the flourishing and powerful Roman Empire.

Marcus and His Teachers

While his adopted father was his illumined guide and mentor in the field of politics and governance, another important figure who influenced Marcus during his youth was his teacher, Fronto. A slew of correspondence between the student and teacher is available even today, giving us a glimpse into the curious mind of Marcus.

The letters reflect a deep and caring student-teacher connection in which both people's genuine need to ask questions and provide illuminating answers are clearly evident. These important letters form the primary source of our knowledge about Fronto's mastery in oratory and language skills.

Fronto's full name was Marcus Cornelius Fronto, and he was a very popular orator, grammarian, and rhetorician during Marcus Aurelius' youth. Emperor Hadrian appointed Fronto to personally tutor Marcus and his cousin, Lucius Verus, who later became co-emperor of the Roman Empire with Marcus Aurelius.

Fronto is credited with reviving the vocabulary and grammar of the old Latin version that was followed by early Roman writers. His teachings and writings are believed to have injected new vitality into Latin prose writings of those times. The student in this student-teacher relationship was a highly intelligent, serious-minded, and hard-working individual.

In addition to the usual Greek and Latin lessons, Marcus Aurelius was keenly interested in learning philosophy, especially Stoicism. In fact, after a while, Marcus got impatient with the constant practices and exercises in advanced Latin and Greek. He was more interested in learning about and embracing the philosophical ideas of Stoicism enumerated by Epictetus; a former slave turned Stoic philosopher.

Marcus is believed to have devoured Epictetus' work titled Diatribai (Discourses) during his student days. The lessons learned at this stage of his life are what guided Marcus right through his life as the Emperor of one of the most powerful empires of those times. The ideals, principles, and values of Epictetus shaped Marcus' spiritual as well as intellectual paths.

Before Fronto came as a tutor into Marcus' life, another teacher Diognetus is believed to have first introduced Marcus to philosophical texts as early as 132 AD when he was just 11 years old. It is believed that Diognetus most likely introduced Marcus to the works of Cynicism. This philosophical school promoted a life of complete frugality regarding all social norms and appearances as being nothing but artifice.

The child Marcus was impressed with the Cynic way of life, choosing to wear a rough woolen cloak as clothing and even slept on the ground in his room instead of his luxurious bed. We know about this because he mentions these incidences in his life in his book Meditations. He talks about how he chose to live the life of a Greek camper after associating with Diognetus and learning about Cynicism and its tenets.

It is quite likely that his mother interfered with his life habits and made him revert to what he was originally being groomed for; to hold an important public office in the Roman Empire in the future.

After this, Fronto Marcus Cornelius Fronto and Herodes Atticus were appointed as tutors to Marcus Aurelius. Both these teachers were highly influential pedagogues in their respective fields of study and charged hefty sums for their skills. While Fronto and Marcus became lifelong friends, Atticus exerted a strong influence on the mind of the future Emperor of Rome.

Marcus and Antoninus

Antoninus was a highly effective monarch of the Roman Empire. Under the able supervision of this indefatigable Emperor and adopted father, Marcus learned and mastered the various aspects of running a government. He was appointed in various public roles by Antoninus. He was the consul three times in 140, 145, and 161 before becoming the Emperor.

Marcus devotes many passages in Meditations in praise of Antoninus and lists multiple impressive qualities he wished to emulate from his father. Emperor Antoninus groomed his young adopted son in all matters of governance and emperorship, except in the field of military campaigns, which almost always the work of generals of the Roman Army.

As he grew older and wiser, Marcus was given an increased amount of political and governing responsibility by his adopted father, Antoninus. He evolved into powerful support for Emperor Antoninus and gave him wise counsel as well. Marcus continued his studies in advanced Latin and Greek. Additionally, his interest in learning and mastering Stoic philosophy did not wane at all. Further, he took a keen interest in law.

Although he lived the life of a future emperor as instructed by Antoninus, it was clear that Marcus

Aurelius was drawn more to philosophy and questions of life than ruling over a vast empire.

In his letters to Fronto, his teacher-turned-best-friend, Marcus complains a lot about his official duties, which he thought were highly clerical in nature. To someone with his philosophical bent of mind, doing the job of a public officer would have seemed meaningless, even if it was one of the most powerful and eminent positions.

During his time of training under his father, Marcus was also introduced to two teachers whose specialty was in the study of philosophy. These two teachers were Apollonius of Chalcedon and Quintus Junius Rusticus. The latter is one of the most influential Stoic philosophers and is revered even today. Marcus highly praises both these philosophers in his Meditations and also talks about the many lessons he learned from them.

He thanks Rusticus for introducing Epictetus' letters to him. It looks like Rusticus loaned his copy of Epictetus' collection of lectures to Marcus for him to read, understand, and master. Further,

Marcus tells us that he learned the importance of independence and reliability, both of which are crucial principles of Stoic philosophy. These entries in his book about his youth are evidence that this was the first time Marcus got introduced to the philosophy of Stoicism.

Chapter Two:

Marcus Aurelius - The Emperor

The story of how Marcus Aurelius came to be anointed the future Emperor of the Roman Empire remains a mystery. Emperor Hadrian reigned between 117 and 138 A.D. In the year 136 A.D., Hadrian announced his successor to be Lucius Ceionius Commodus, who was given the official title of L. Aelius Caesar.

In the same year, Marcus was engaged to be married to Commodus' daughter Ceionia Fabia. Commodus died closely followed by the death of Emperor Hadrian. After the death of Commodus and Hadrian in 138 A.D, the engagement was canceled. In 138 A.D., Marcus married Emperor Antoninus' daughter, Annia Galeria Faustina, later on in 145.

But, before he died, Hadrian appointed Titus Aurelius Antoninus as his successor. He also made Antoninus adopt Marcus Aurelius as his son and named him the successor after Antoninus.

Additionally, Hadrian made Antoninus adopt Commodus' son, Lucius Verus, as well. This point plays an important role in one of the future decisions that Marcus Aurelius takes after he becomes Emperor. Therefore, Marcus' destiny as the Emperor of Rome was sealed when he was just 17 years old. Antoninus ascended the throne in 138 A.D. and ruled until he died in 161 A.D.

Thus, Marcus had to wait for nearly 23 years before he became Emperor of Rome. In fact, some historians believe that Hadrian was merely using Commodus and Antoninus only as 'place-warmers' to the Roman throne for Marcus Aurelius and/or Lucius Verus.

In the year 147 A.D., Marcus was formally conferred the powers of emperorship, namely the imperium and Tribunicia Potestas. From 147 onwards, Marcus was like a junior emperor playing a crucial supporting role to Emperor Antoninus. He participated in all the intimate council meetings and took part in all the decisions taken by the Emperor.

By this time, Marcus' adopted brother and the second adopted son of Antoninus, Lucius Verus, was also brought into the power circle. Marcus and

Verus were joint consuls when Emperor Antoninus died in 161. The transition of emperorship to Marcus Aurelius was smooth and uneventful, considering that he already had essential powers conferred on him four years ago.

In 161, after the death of Emperor Antoninus, Marcus Aurelius took on the full constitutional powers of the Roman Empire. Henceforth, Marcus was officially known as Imperator Caesar Marcus Aurelius Antoninus Augustus. However, there was a twist to this tale that happened under the insistence of the new Emperor.

Marcus insisted that his adopted brother be crowned co-emperor along with him. And so, Lucius Verus was anointed joint Emperor with Marcus and bore the official title of Imperator Caesar Lucius Aurelius Verus Augustus.

The brothers together ascended the throne of the Roman Empire, and they started their governance by setting up programs for the upliftment of the poor. They also undertook the task of enhancing the rewards for the Roman army by increasing salaries and by giving the soldiers greater honor than before.

Other important measures are taken by the new joint emperors of the Roman Empire included:

- Encouragement of free speech
- Improved arts and education in the Empire
- Boosted the economy by debasing the currency

All these new and innovative measures of the joint emperors made them highly popular among the Romans. The interesting factor in this combination is that Lucius Verus did not seem to have any popular fan following among the subjects. A ruthless co-ruler could have easily gotten rid of him. The fact that Marcus Aurelius did not choose this option, and on the other hand, insisted on making his adopted brother a co-emperor speaks volumes of the power and depth of his moral strength character.

However, some historians beg to have a different view of this situation. They feel Marcus proposed Lucius Verus' name as co-emperor because he was assuaged by his own conscience. He believed that Emperor Hadrian wanted this to happen, which is why the late Emperor insisted that Antoninus adopt both Marcus and Lucius and train them for the upcoming job.

Whatever was the reason or compulsion behind Marcus' decision, this situation was a first in the history of the Roman Empire; two emperors holding equal constitutional powers and statuses. However, all historians agree that the achievements of Lucius Verus were far smaller and fewer than those of Marcus Aurelius.

Yet, some historians believe that Marcus may not have been able to do everything in his vast Empire by himself and that his co-emperor, Lucius Verus, would likely have contributed to the running of the Roman Empire.

The most significant contribution of Marcus Aurelius to the Roman Empire was in the field of law, an area that he was most interested in. Multiple new and innovative legal measures were put in place, and numerous judicial matters were settled during the reign of Marcus Aurelius.

An interesting point of difference existed between the lives of the joint Roman emperors. Even after becoming the Emperor, Marcus stuck to leading a simple, philosophical life based on the principles of Stoic disciplines. On the other hand, Lucius Verus, who was always used to a life of luxury and extravagance, increased the lavishness in his life after becoming Emperor.

Verus threw lavish parties for his friends and gave them expensive gifts as well. There is a particularly notorious story of one such lavish party hosted by Verus for his friends and family. There is a record of it in Historia Augusta. According to this record, Verus hosted a party in which return gifts for his friends were in the form of gold and silver bowls embedded with stunning gems, carriages designed with silver harnesses, gold vases shaped like perfume boxes, and more.

The Historia Augusta also records that, when Marcus Aurelius heard of this extravagant party, he groaned and wept agonizingly, thinking about the fate of the Roman Empire.

Marcus Aurelius is himself best remembered for eliminating harshness and cruel, punitive measures and various anomalies in civil law. His legal policies helped in improving the condition of the less privileged sections of Roman society, including minors, widows, and slaves. He was known as a sympathetic ombudsman helping to solve problems of the lower sections of the society.

Wars and Battles of the Roman Empire Under the Stewardship of Marcus Aurelius

In 161, the Parthians invaded Syria, a powerful and important economic center of the Roman Empire. The Parthians were led by King Vologases, who actually attacked Armenia, which was under the control of the Roman Empire. The province of Syria decided to retaliate by attacking King Vologases' army.

As Lucius Verus was more experienced in military campaigns than Marcus, he took charge of the wars on the eastern front. The war between the Romans and Parthians lasted from 162 to 166 and was mostly under the command of Lucius Verus. Another individual who played a notable role in winning this was for the Roman Empire was General Gaius Avidius Cassius. In fact, historians believed that it was the brilliant military strategy of Cassius and the excellent way he deployed Roman troops that actually won the war for the Roman Empire.

While Verus was on the eastern frontier fighting battles for Rome, Marcus Aurelius remained in Rome and performed his duties diligently. He heard court cases and passed judgments. He reviewed and passed laws that benefited all sections of society in Rome, especially the less privileged sections. Marcus also faced and dealt with multiple requests and problems that came in from the various provinces of the Roman Empire.

It was during this period between 162 and 166 A.D. that Marcus Aurelius is believed to have persecuted followers of a then-new religion, namely Christianity. In retrospect and on Christianity's triumph, this action of Marcus was condemned by many people. However, it is now seen as an important step the Emperor needed to take against people who didn't follow the state religion to keep the peace.

By 166 A.D., the war with the Parthians was over, and the Christian problem was sorted out too. By this time, he and his wife Faustina, whom he married in 145, had many children. Even if many of his children died quite young, Marcus believed that the universe was smiling on him, and he is going to be happy and at peace.

However, Marcus' problems were far from over. The army, led by Verus against the Parthians, returned to their homeland happy and victorious. However, they brought a plague that devastated a large portion of the Roman population for several years after. The problems of the plague were exacerbated by German invasions, and these two catastrophes together weakened the morale of not just the soldiers of the Roman army but also the entire Empire, which, hitherto, had gotten accustomed to long periods of peace, prosperity, and stability.

Both the Roman emperors set out in a military campaign across the Danube. However, while they were busy here, numerous tribes from Germany invaded Italy. They laid siege over Aquileia, an important commercial and military center of the Roman Empire situated at the head of the Adriatic coast.

These German invasions actually began around 150 before Marcus became Emperor. In 150, a large German tribe called Marcomanni started migrating to the south of the Danube River towards the middle of the Danube region. From this year onwards, Marcus was engaged in battles with Germans as he continued his efforts to prevent them from making inroads into the Roman Empire.

During the time of Marcus' German campaigns in the Danube region, the Roman Empire was in a very precarious state. Their military prowess and financial powers, which were hitherto unquestioned, were suddenly seen as highly vulnerable in the eyes of the world. To ease the financial burden of the Roman Empire, multiple royal properties were auctioned and sold off, which helped in filling the coffers.

Verus and Marcus were able to win the war against the Germans, at least for the time being. But, Lucius Verus died of a stroke in 169, and Marcus was left alone to continue fighting for three more years before he could restore the Danube region to the Roman Empire. It took another three years of battle before Marcus was able to bring peace among the tribes that lived beyond the Danube frontiers.

While Marcus was busy securing the Roman borders of the Danube frontiers, the other regions of the Empire, including Britain, Egypt, and Spain, were plagued by external invasions as well as internal rebellions. General Gaius Avidius Cassius, who fought under Lucius Verus, was becoming all-powerful and almost made himself prefect of the eastern regions of the Roman Empire. Egypt, especially, was a very important province of the Roman Empire, and Cassius took control of this region. Moreover, fanned by rumors about Marcus' death, General Gaius Avidius Cassius proclaimed himself Emperor of the Roman Empire.

At this juncture, Marcus made peace with those tribes in the Danube region that he had not yet subjugated under the Roman rule and marched towards the east to confront General Gaius Avidius Cassius. But before he could do anything, Marcus got the news that General Cassius was murdered by his own soldiers.

Despite hearing this news while on his way to the eastern regions, Marcus chose to continue in that direction. He converted the military campaign into a tour to inspect and pacify the troubled areas in the eastern part of the Roman Empire. Marcus visited many places, including Athens, Antioch, and Alexandria.

His biggest loss during this part of his journey was the death of his wife, Faustina, who had accompanied him in the military campaign to the Danube frontiers. Faustina received accolades for her support in her husband's work in life, as well as in death. Marcus talks about his wife's love and devotion to him in his journals.

In 177, Marcus named his son, Commodus, as co-emperor. Both father and son continued the Danubian military campaigns. However, this time, Marcus chose an offensive attitude instead of an earlier defensive attack. He also intended to expand the northern territories of the Roman Empire during these campaigns with his son.

He achieved a lot of success in his expansionist endeavor until he died in 180, at the military headquarters in the Danube frontiers. Just before he died, he made sure that his chief advisers knew that he wanted his son Commodus to succeed him.

As an emperor, Marcus' choice of his son as his successor is seen as a paradox. The reason for this view is that he was known for his philosophical outlook right through his life, not chasing any personal ambitions or desires and doing everything from the view of being the Emperor of one of the largest empires in the world.

Choosing his son as successor was seen by some as changing her perspective from a philosophical to a dynastic perspective, where he appeared to be keen on saving the legacy of his family instead of following the example of choosing the 'best man' for the role. Some historians debate this point of view, saying that Marcus really did not have a choice in the matter because if he didn't name his son as successor, he was quite likely to have been put to death.

If his son Commodus who reigned from 180 to 192, was a better emperor than he turned out to be, maybe these allegations on Marcus Aurelius may not have come by at all. However, sadly, Commodus' reign was a forgettable one in the history of the Roman Empire. In fact, his reign more or less set the path for the complete declination of the Empire.

Marcus' failure to make his son as worthy as his adopted father Antoninus made him reflects a popular maxim of the Roman Emperor found in his work Meditations. The maxim goes something like this; "What cannot or does not transmit light creates its own darkness."

Marcus' reign was rife with war and diseases, unlike the period of the previous reign under Emperor Antoninus, which was a period of peace and prosperity. He, along with his brother and co-emperor Verus, was caught in back-to-back military conquests. Like a true Stoic, Marcus never wavered from the call of duty and, unlike earlier Roman emperors who left the actual fighting to the generals, took up arms and went on military campaigns relentlessly, sometimes to quell rebellions, and sometimes intending to expand the territories of the Roman Empire.

Even though a large period of his reign was entangled in multiple military campaigns, Marcus is best remembered for his contemplative character and his keenness in using reason and logic to rule over the Roman Empire. Despite being busy with wars and battles of the Roman Empire, Marcus Aurelius found the time to establish four Chairs of Philosophy in Athens, one each for the philosophies of Epicurean, Aristotelian, Platonic, and Stoic.

Chapter Three:

A Brief History of Stoicism

If you try to understand the history and legacy of Marcus Aurelius, Emperor of Rome, without studying Stoicism and his contributions to this field of philosophy, then your work is only half-done. The histories of this Roman Emperor and Stoicism are forever intertwined. So, before we go into what Marcus Aurelius contributed to Stoicism, let us equip ourselves with a brief history of Stoicism.

Understanding Stoicism

According to the philosophical approach of the Stoics, attaining eudaimonia (sometimes spelled as eudaemonia) is the ultimate goal in life. This state of ultimate Stoic enlightenment is leading a contented and flourishing life. Stoicism exhorts followers to achieve eudaemonia by living in accordance with and aligning their lives with nature.

How does one define a life aligned with nature? According to Stoicism, this feat can be achieved by fulfilling your purpose in the entire universal scheme. It means that you live as per your providence and destiny. Another important point of difference that Stoicism points out between human beings and other living creatures is our ability to reason and think logically.

Therefore, if we are endowed with this special power of reason, then it is destined that we use it effectively. Reason and logic are the primary bases on which a true Stoic chooses to make all decisions in life. Human beings are mandated by nature to act logically and rationally and not give in to emotions, a state defined as apatheia in Stoicism.

Stoics believe that external circumstances cannot and should not be categorized as good or bad. The best way of dealing with external factors is to be indifferent to them. Instead, we must make every choice of our life through the use of reason and rationality, regardless of what the external circumstances appear to tell us.

The path leading to eudaimonia has been developed through thousands of years by multiple leaders and practitioners of Stoicism. The Golden Period of Stoicism is believed to have happened between 300 B.C. and 200 A.D. lasting more than five centuries. Let us look in brief at the various stages of this Golden Era of Stoicism and the people. Their contributions have significantly impacted the growth and development of this field of philosophy.

The development of Stoicism is typically divided into three periods, namely:

1. The Early Stoa
2. The Middle Stoa
3. The Late Stoa

Our knowledge about the Late Stoa period is the most extensive considering numerous works of that time are extant today. However, based on the writings that we have from the Late Stoa, historians have been able to stitch together a reasonably accurate picture of the Early and the Middle Stoa.

The Early Stoa (300 to 100 B.C.)

The School of Stoicism was established in Athens in 300 B.C. by Zeno of Citium. Ideas of Stoicism were created primarily to oppose the philosophical concepts of Epicureanism, another school of philosophy founded around the same time by Epicurus. According to Epicurus, our world is materialistic and accidental in character and is driven by emotions of pleasure and pain. Stoicism took a contrary stand to this supposition.

Zeno developed Stoicism by taking ideas from Cynicism and multiple other philosophical schools that flourished during his time in Greece. He proposed that leading a life of simplicity and virtue can help in achieving happiness and contentment.

Zeno started his school in the Stoa Poikile or the Painted Porch, a covered colonnade in the central marketplace of Athens. This place was accessible to the public, and everyone who was interested could join in the philosophical discussions of Zeno. The name Stoicism, as evident, has its roots in the Greek word 'Stoa' or porch.

Zeno's influence in setting up the new branch of philosophy was huge. He distinguished his theory of Stoicism into three sections, including physics, logic, and ethics. While the founder insisted on the equal importance of all three, today, Stoicism is relegated only to ethics.

Cleanthes, Zeno's student, took over the principalship of the school of Stoicism after his master's death. He ensured the principles of Zeno were maintained even though he did not add anything new or significant to the existing tenets and principles. The third head, or scholarch, of Zeno's Stoic school of Philosophy, was Chrysippus of Soli. This Stoic did a lot of work to expand the three parts of Stoicism by developing a system referred to as propositional logic.

Chrysippus of Soli gets the credit of establishing his master's school of philosophy as one of the foremost and popular schools, not only in ancient Greece but also in the history of philosophy. After Chrysippus, the Stoic school was led by three people whose names are still spoken with respect in the field of philosophy even if their contributions were far less significant than those of their more eminent predecessors. These three were Zeno of Tarsus, Diogenes of Babylon, and Antipater of Tarsus.

The Middle Stoa (100 B.C. 1 A.D.)

Until around 100 B.C., Stoicism remained in Greece. From around 100 B.C., it began to spread to Rome as well. Panaetius was the seventh head of the Stoic school of philosophy, founded by Zeno of Citium. Panaetius was quite flexible in accepting new norms into the principles and ideals of Stoicism than Zeno and the other predecessors.

He reduced the complexities involved in the physics and logic aspects of Stoicism and focused more on ethics. This paradigm shift resulted in Stoicism resembling Neoplatonism, which was already quite popular in ancient Rome. Therefore, it became easy to introduce the new format of Stoicism into Rome.

An important event during the Middle Stoa is that Panaetius is considered the last scholarch of Zeno's Stoicism. This is because, after his time, there was no single unified school of Stoicism as Zeno made it out to be. But the various tenets and principles of Stoicism introduced by Zeno continued to flourish across the Roman Empire.

The next important Stoic during the Middle Stoa period was Posidonius, who reinforced the altered ideas proposed by Panaetius. Moreover, he moved Stoicism closer to the ideals of Plato and Aristotle.

Important and prominent Romans who embraced Stoicism during the Middle Stoa included Cicero and Cato the Younger. Cato the Younger was especially famous for his austere way of life and his uncompromising outlook on the absolute importance of moral integrity. In fact, some historians think that Cato the Younger was closer to the founder of Stoicism, Zeno of Citium, than Panaetius and Posidonius, both of whom created a more eclectic form of Stoicism deriving and embracing values and principles from Neoplatonism and Aristotelianism.

The Late Stoa (1 A.D. - 200 A.D.)

Thanks to the efforts of Posidonius and Panaetius, Stoicism in the Roman Empire consisted primarily of ethics, with both physics and logic being almost not studied at all. For the modern-day historian and philosopher, it appeared from writings of the time that survived, that the period of the Late Stoa was the most vibrant time for Stoicism. The three most important contributors to our understanding of Stoicism in the Late Stoa include Seneca, Epictetus, and Marcus Aurelius.

Seneca, the Younger's writings consist of a collection of letters titled Epistulae morales ad Lucilium or Moral Letters to Lucilius. These letters consist of explanations of moral lessons based on day-to-day routine events. Seneca's works are admired for the unique writing style, and even today, his ideas are read avidly by people all around the world.

Epictetus is the second Stoic philosopher belonging to the Late Stoa whose works include Discourses and Enchiridion (or the Handbook). Epictetus' works and writings had a huge impact on the most famous Stoic philosopher of all time, namely Marcus Aurelius, the philosopher-king of the Roman Empire.

As you already know by now, the most famous work of Marcus Aurelius' is Meditations, which he had titled as Ta eis heauton or To Himself. Today, there is little doubt that Mediations is the most widely read and discussed work on Stoicism and its tenets. Marcus speaks about self-discipline, reason, moral integrity, and the idea of world citizenship in his journals.

His ideas continue to inspire the modern man. In fact, Marcus is seen to be a role model for many of us in terms of personal growth and development. He is considered to be the last prominent Stoic belonging to the Late Stoa. Therefore, it is easy to understand why Marcus and Stoicism are inseparable.

Chapter Four:

Marcus Aurelius - The Philosopher-King

Now that we know about Marcus Aurelius' wars and battles, it is time to focus on the element he is best remembered for, namely his philosophical outlook to his emperorship. Nearly all historians and philosophers agree that Marcus Aurelius was a practicing Stoic. Marcus himself refers to many Stoics before and during his lifetime who had a tremendous impact on his philosophical outlook. He mentions the name of Rusticus from whom he seems to have borrowed the book, Discourses, written by the slave-turned-philosopher, Epictetus.

And yet, he does not call himself a Stoic in any part of Meditations. This could be because he never intended for his writings to be read or heard by an audience. He was only writing a journal for his personal use and not to define himself in any way to any kind of audience.

Despite his evident liking for Stoicism and its tenets, Marcus was also open to the philosophical ideas of other schools that flourished in Rome during that time. The fact that he established four Chairs of Philosophy in Athens for Platonism, Aristotelianism, Epicureanism, and Stoicism clearly demonstrate his openness to learn and understand other philosophical ideas as well. This action also proves that Marcus did not blindly follow the tenets of Stoicism in his personal life. He had heard, read, and understood other ideas and only then decided to make Stoicism his way of life.

Influence of Epictetus on Marcus Aurelius

There is little doubt that Marcus Aurelius knew and appreciated a lot of philosophical ideas of Epictetus, considering that the Emperor quotes the slave-turned-philosopher multiple times in Meditations. In 2 A.D., the popularity and fame of Epictetus' and his Stoic ideals are believed to have been more than those of Plato. He has been hailed as the greatest Stoic of all times by numerous experts.

Now, it goes to say that if Marcus Aurelius were attracted to Stoicism, then he would definitely have been influenced by the highly-acclaimed Epictetus. Therefore, it makes sense to understand the tenets of Epictetus' Stoicism first. This basic understanding will help us to explore and appreciate the ideas in Marcus Aurelius' Meditations.

The Three Topoi

The primary and core principle of Epictetus' Stoicism was centered on the Three Topoi or the three aspects of Stoicism that are needed to understand the philosophy in its entirety fully. According to Discourses, these Three Topoi include:

- The impulse to take action or hormas and not to take action or aphormas

- Aversions or ekkliseis and desires or orexeis

- Freedom from anything connected with assents or sunkatatheseis, including hasty judgments and deception

These three aspects of Epictetus' ideals correspond to the founding philosopher Zeno's three subjects of study, namely physics, ethics, and logic. Epictetus believed not just in theoretical philosophy but wanted his tenets to be applied to daily life and its routines, including simple to complex decision-making processes.

Epictetus believed that students of philosophy should apply their theoretical knowledge to practical everyday use so that they could transform their lives positively. Only this path would make an apprentice philosopher into a sage (Sophos) or a truly wise man. The three topoi that Epictetus ordained were to help learners achieve this end.

The aversion-desire tenet is related to physics. According to Epictetus, a true philosopher must not only know how nature works but also train his desires and aversions in such a way that they are aligned and harmonious with the ways of nature. Stoics believe that nature is a complex set of interconnected systems of physics and identified with the divine. Human beings are merely a part of this intricate and complex system of nature.

According to Epictetus Stoicism, if an individual has desires and aversions that conflict with the ways of larger physical systems of nature, then he is bound to encounter frustration and sadness. Therefore, to become a sage as defined by Stoicism, we must train ourselves to have only those desires that are aligned with nature's systems and workings.

The impulse of action or inaction is connected with ethics. Epictetus believed that while the study of theoretical ethics is important to become a sage, it is equally important to train our impulses and behaviors so that we may take ethical action in practical, everyday life. So, a learner of Stoicism must not only study theory but also apply the lessons of ethics to his daily life, and this approach is what will help him reach the state of a wise sage.

The tenet of assents is connected with logic. Epictetus believed that every impression that we form consists of a subjective value-judgment aspect of each individual. He warns that when we give our assent to any of our impressions, we also agree to the individualistic value-judgment aspect that forms part of the impression. For example, if we see someone eating more than what we believe he should, then we form the impression that the person is eating excessively. This belief is a result of our value-judgment and not necessarily factually correct about the person who is eating.

Therefore, Epictetus warns followers and learners of Stoicism to be on guard against falling prey to such individual-based and unwarranted value-judgments and use only logic, reason, and facts to give assent. A novice philosopher needs to spend time and energy to train himself consistently and persistently to achieve this end.

In conclusion, it can be summarized that Epictetus urged his followers to not only master the theory of Stoicism but train themselves to implement the mastered theories in their daily life. Historians and philosophers believe that Marcus considered himself to be a student of Epictetus. Therefore, a brief understanding of the slave-turned-philosopher's ideas is important to comprehend and appreciate the personal notes found in Marcus' Meditations.

Chapter Five:

Meditations - Summary and Significance

The intimate connection with Marcus' thoughts to modern-day philosophy lies in his collection of daily writings titled 'Meditations.' In fact, the philosopher-kings reputation as a philosopher rests entirely on this work. This collection of writings is actually like a personal journal or notebook in which the Roman emperor regularly wrote while on his military campaigns in Central Europe. Some historians might not treat this source as being 'historically accurate' considering that it consists of 'thoughts and ideas' and not necessarily facts.

It is not clear whether these writings were meant for others to read at all because there is no real structure to the entire work. Some historians believe that these notes were written by the Emperor as a self-help mechanism to prepare himself for the tough challenges he faced each day throughout his administrative and military campaigns.

Meditations is a work that is a collection of many things. It has short quotes and sayings and long passages as well. It is not really organized into any kind of theme or category. However, certain ideas keep repeating in the book, reflecting the importance these ideas were to Marcus.

Yet, the study of Marcus Aurelius from a historical point of view would be incomplete if we don't read and understand the Emperor's thoughts. His ideas and thoughts penned in his personal diary have inspired and motivated people throughout history. Another interesting feature of this collection of thoughts is that the Roman Emperor wrote them in Greek, reflecting the extent to which the union of the Greek and Roman cultures had already taken place by them.

Through his journals, Marcus exhorts and encourages himself to self-actualize. He continually impresses upon himself to achieve exceedingly high levels of moral conduct, analyzing the physical trivialities of the human world. He continually talks about the importance of doing one's duty and service.

His collection of works is referred to as the "thoughts of a philosopher-king" and reflects the ethos and thinking process of society at the time. Yet, there is little doubt that the ideas of the Roman Emperor were not really his own but borrowed from the philosophy of Stoicism.

His ideas are all based on the moral tenets of Stoicism, which Marcus learned and mastered by reading and imbibing the works of Epictetus (50 - 135A.D), a slave-turned-Stoic-philosopher. The tenets of Stoicism that Marcus Aurelius tried to implement in his own life include the following ideas:

- The entire universe is interconnected and governed by an element referred to as 'intelligence.'

- The human soul is derived from this divine intelligence.

- Therefore, the human soul can, if it chooses, stand pure and untouched by the problems of chaos and futility that surround it.

The first recorded mention of Marcus Aurelius' Meditations was found in a work of Themistius written in 364. Themistius calls it Marcus' precepts or parangelmata. In 900, the Suidas, which is a Byzantine encyclopedia of ancient history, calls Marcus' work an agoge, which means directing or leading. In the 10th century, Bishop Arethas of Caesarea labeled it as 'writings to himself' in one of his manuscripts, which is now lost.

Today, nearly all historians agree that the notes of Marcus were meant as a way of self-improvement in morality. He used his journals to remind himself of important Stoic doctrines that he wanted to emulate in his life or when faced with difficult choices. He talks about how life is governed by Fate or Providence and how the power of happiness lies in virtue, and living a virtuous life is entirely in our hands.

The current texts of Meditations are primarily derived from two sources. One is an old manuscript held in the Vatican archives, and the second is the lost manuscript of Bishop Arethas of Caesarea. The first edition of the current form of Marcus Aurelius' book was printed in 1558.

Brief Summary of Meditations

The entire book is divided into 12 short books, and here is a brief summary of what each of these smaller books contains.

Book 1 - In this book, Marcus Aurelius thanks all the people to whom he felt indebted. Here are some of the things he thanks the various people in his life for:

- Grandfather - for teaching him the importance of and how to be modest, candid, and even-tempered.

- Father - for teaching him how to be frugal, calm, and humble. He also learned the art of unwavering adherence to decisions made after deliberations and thorough investigations. His father also taught him to be indifferent to external and superfluous honors. He learned from his father the important lesson of when to push and when to back off in difficult situations.

- Mother - for teaching him the art of generosity and the value of having a non-materialistic outlook in life.

- Teachers - for teaching him, in addition to the various subjects, the importance of self-discipline, hard work, rationality, equanimity, tolerance, and humor. He also thanks his teachers for having taught him to come outside of mere theoretical metaphysics and make philosophy a way of life.

He thanks them for his love of practical philosophy instead of being stuck at mastering theory alone like many of the other philosophers of that time. His teachers taught him not to take sides with any fighter in games and chariot races, to learn to handle and put up with discomforts, have no demands from others, and continue doing work ensuring not to waste time and energy on slanderers.

- Wife - for being affectionate and loving.

Book 2 - In this book, Marcus reminds himself not to be angry at people who cause him pain or hurt him in any way. He tells himself that all human beings are imperfect, and therefore, we must not be angry with others for their imperfection. He says that human beings are nothing but bits of flesh, bones, blood, and breath. Our life is fleeting, and we will all decay and die.

Also, he tells himself that there is nothing to fear about death because it cannot and will not hurt us. The most important element in human beings is our mind. If we can control our minds from becoming slaves to selfishness, worthless desires and passions, and not battle with fate, then our purpose is served.

We have to teach our minds to be calm and not get anxious about how things are turning out right now or will turn out in the future. If we can keep our minds calm and free from worry, then this state is far superior to both pleasure and pain. Freedom for human beings lies in controlling our minds.

Book 3 - In this book, Marcus reminds himself to be mindful of every little thing that he experiences through his senses. For example, he tells us (as he tells himself) to be observant and watch out for little things like cracks in a loaf of bread, the wonderful texture of olives and figs, and even the expressions of wild animals. He says that all these seemingly mundane elements around us have charm and beauty.

In Book 3, Marcus warns against spending time and energy over useless and harmful gossip. He also tells us how important it is not to spend your life worrying and speculating about what others are thinking of you. Instead, Marcus advises, we must spend our time talking only about those things that we will not be ashamed of if it is discovered by others.

For example, he urges us to talk about positive things like cheerfulness, sincerity, etc. He says that by discussing such positive things, a certain kind of divinity will light up within us. Marcus believes that nothing is more valuable than a mind that seeks justice, truth, forbearance, temperance, and rationality. Therefore, Book 3 of Meditations is focused on helping himself (and the readers) to pursue good.

Book 4 - In this book, Marcus talks about where to find peace. He says that peace is in our own minds. If we can keep our mind clear and calm, then we can easily find happiness and peace. He urges us not to dwell on what others think of us because, in reality, we have no control over this element.

He tells us that if others agree or not, if we do a virtuous act, then nobody can change it because virtue remains virtue whether others acknowledge it or not. He reminds us of the ephemerality of life. We are alive in one instant, and we are dead the next instant. Therefore, it is our duty to lead a virtuous and happy life knowing and accepting that we have very little time on our hands. If we live like this, then when it is time for us to be dropped from the tree of life, we will be dropped like a ripe fruit.

Book 5 - In Book 5, Marcus encourages us to get up each morning and see what good we can do to others. We should act and behave in a way that is aligned with nature and should not hesitate to contribute to society without fear of reproach from others. Also, he says that we must not expect payment or something in return for our good work. Instead, we must find happiness in just doing good works. Marcus asks us to be like the vine that bears sweet fruits for others, even though it cannot partake of the fruits. Being virtuous is a reward by itself.

Book 6 - In this book, Marcus speaks aggressively against the idea of vengeance. He believes that there is no point in repeating and copying injuries and reiterating the importance of fulfilling our duties and acting righteously. He instills the cruciality of learning to be unperturbed by the behaviors and reactions of others around us.

He reminds us again that in the infinite vastness of time and space in the whole cosmos, human beings are significant, and our emotions are even less significant than ourselves. Therefore, we must shed feelings of anger and revenge and just focus on performing our duties righteously. Marcus says in his sixth book that our primary focus should be to control our minds and fill it with positive thoughts.

Book 7 - In this seventh book, Marcus talks highly about the power of tolerance and patience. He says that nature works like wax. It is continually shaping and reshaping things, and therefore, we have to wait patiently and tolerate our problems.

Regardless of what we do, people will always discover bad things to speak about us. But, we have to develop the power of tolerance towards such people. Evil and bad people will always find a means to try out tolerance and patience. But, we must learn to counter these moves and remain happy by controlling how we respond to them.

Book 8 - In Book 8, he argues against attempts to disconnect with humanity. He calls this exercise as futile because disconnecting with humanity is like cutting off our own limbs. So, instead of this futile effort, we must learn to connect with nature as well as other people around us.

Regardless of whom or what we encounter, we must maintain a calm, serene, and dignified countenance, and this is possible only if we learn to control our minds. He uses the analogy of spring to explain the uselessness of returning a curse with a curse. He asks that if we curse spring, will it have any effect on springtime. Similarly, we must learn not to be affected by the curses of other people.

Book 9, 10, and 11 - The theme of these three books is common. Marcus Aurelius talks about the importance of moderation, sincerity, honesty, and calmness in all our interactions with other people. If someone accuses you of not being virtuous, we must learn to disregard such notions from our head and continue doing good work. Marcus also urges people to use humor to handle such aggressions against your morality.

Book 12 - In this last book, Marcus asks a very pertinent question. He says that there is no doubt that every human being loves himself the most. And yet, we put our own opinions about ourselves below those of others. Why do we have this conflicting behavior? He says that this conflict is a mistake, and we must endeavor not to get embroiled in it. We must be true to ourselves and ensure that we behave in the right way regardless of what others think of us.

He also reminds us that good and evil people meet the same end. Everyone turns to ashes in the end. Therefore, Marcus believes that it is best to lead a life of humility instead of arrogance and pride. With such behavior, we can die in peace.

The fact that Marcus Aurelius repeats many of his ideas multiple times in his book demonstrates the way of life of a true Stoic. Stoicism is essentially journaling our thoughts and ideas, repeating them in our minds so that our mind is habituating into this way of thinking.

Stoicism is about repeatedly reminding ourselves of the standards we have set for our lives and finding ways and means to live up to these standards. These repetitive exercises are very useful, especially in those times when we feel morally inadequate, unsure, or weak-minded.

Marcus is no just philosophizing when he talks about death and the awareness it creates about the fleetingness of human beings. He uses this knowledge and urges himself and us to use this fact in all our decision-making and our perspectives.

Philosophical Exercises in Meditations

The ideas and thoughts found in Marcus Aurelius' Meditations are quite unique in the sense that you are unlikely to find similar ones in the works of other great Greek and Roman philosophers of that time, including Aristotle or even Hierocles, another Stoic who lived around the same time as the philosopher-king.

To reiterate a point said earlier, Meditations was written by Marcus for himself, for his own use and any specific audience. This work is not a theoretical treatise that speaks either for or against any doctrine. The function of this book is quite different from other philosophical treatises. And, to understand this functionality of Meditations, we must know a little bit about an element called "philosophical exercises" or askêsis.

Right through his journal, Marcus is engaged in multiple philosophical exercises that are designed to transform his personality and behavior to reflect the learned stoical theories so that his entire life changed for the better. Marcus repeatedly engaged with stoical ideas. The act of writing them down further helped to habituate his mind to think differently.

This approach is not the same as creating theoretical treatises arguing either in favor or against a said doctrine. Marcus' work is a detailed record of his practical training designed to inculcate philosophical theories into habit-forming practices and exercises.

Using the three kinds of philosophical training suggested by Epictetus, Marcus Aurelius designed and made notes of various combinations of physical, ethical, and logical ideas in his daily journal. The writing down of philosophical ideas is considered to be the second stage of implemented theoretical philosophy in practical life.

The activity of writing down philosophical ideals outlined by Epictetus, Marcus hoped to transform his soul, which, in turn, would positively change his behavior and external attitude. Therefore, the second stage in the life of an apprentice philosopher is to train himself through reflection, putting learned theories into practice to reach the ultimate goal - attaining wisdom and becoming a sage.

Marcus' Ideas on the Cosmos

The most significant philosophical idea that repeatedly appears in Marcus' journal is the concept of the 'cosmos.' The philosopher-king continually exhorts himself to avoid having an individualistic perspective, and instead, view everything that is happening around him through a larger, cosmic perspective.

He believed that human beings have the power to strip away superfluous troubles caused merely because of our value-judgment based perspectives. He believed that human beings are empowered to embrace the limitless cosmos, to perceive rapid changes in multiple working parts of the cosmos, and to look at how short the time available to us between our birth and death is in comparison to the infinite time of the cosmos.

Marcus repeatedly talks about the judgmental attitude of human beings, which is the primary cause of our unhappiness and frustration. He was also inspired by Epictetus' belief that good and evil are products of our judgmental perspectives. According to Epictetus, the frustration of human beings is not rooted in the things themselves as much as it is in the way we perceive those things.

He believed in Epictetus' epistemological ideals as well, wherein impressions created in the minds of people about the nature of things are complex, layered, and composite. The impressions include the perception of an external object combined with an unconscious and involuntary individualistic value-judgment about the object. These value-judgments are formed by our thinking habits as well as preconceived notions about the perceived object.

Nearly all human beings give their assent to these highly complex and composite impressions created in our minds. These assents end up becoming deep-seated beliefs. The job of a philosopher is to rigorously examine the impressions formed in his mind to ensure there are no traces of individualistic biases and other judgmental factors before giving his assent.

According to Epictetus, it is the crucial job of a philosopher to leave out all unwarranted value-judgments before approving his impressions.

This approach will help him see everything in its natural light without being colored by his own opinion, belief systems, and other aspects that could take away the essential truth of the object in question.

Further, Epictetus believed that the binding force of the entire universe is logos, which caused everything here to work harmoniously. A philosopher has to concentrate on his logos to understand how and why everything that happens in the universe is natural. It is only our interpretations that are colored by our value-judgments that make things appear 'good' or 'bad.' Therefore, Epictetus urged his followers to focus on nothing else except the logos to find peace and harmony in their lives.

Marcus followed Epictetus' recommendation about forming impressions diligently. In his Meditations, Marcus noted down a series of philosophical exercises using which he tried to analyze his impressions and get rid of unwarranted value-judgments before taking any decision or agreeing to the impressions formed in his mind.

One of the philosophical exercises he used goes something like this: "Do not analyze anything beyond the first impression report. Otherwise, your own value-judgment will get added and alter this first impression needlessly."

Marcus believed that "first impressions" are the ones that are free of value-judgments, and therefore, as close to the truth as possible. Marcus also believed that the achievement of eudaimonia or the ultimate form of wisdom is highly dependent on forming correct, unprejudiced impressions. This was done through a rigorous and diligent examination of our ideas and thoughts before agreeing or disagreeing with them.

Marcus believed that to live in harmony with nature and achieve eudaimonia, a man must remove unwarranted value-judgments, such as the importance given to an individual's social standing, and wealth which drives all of us to compete with one another.

Such a man can experience the oneness and interconnectedness of the cosmos and see the futility in conflict and destruction. Such a man will be able to identify with the divine. Nearly all the philosophical exercises mentioned in Marcus Aurelius' book are designed to achieve the ultimate experience of the unified cosmos.

What happened to Marcus' journals after his death is not known. It seems to have survived through copies that were made and preserved. The text finds mention in Historia Augusta and the works of Themistius, an acclaimed orator from Rome, in 4 A.D. After this, there is no mention of Marcus' writings until the 10th century when Arethas, the cleric, talks about it in a letter to his friend and even copies it for him.

Aretha's copy could be the reason for the preservation of Meditations, which is believed to have been part of the collection of writings and books rescued in 1453 A.D. from the library of Constantinople just before the city fell into the hands of the Ottoman Turks.

These rescued books were taken to the west where they were copied. By 1559, the first printed edition of Meditations was made available. Since then, this book has been a source of inspiration for many people around the world, most of whom viewed Marcus Aurelius first as a philosopher, and only second as an emperor, a rare thing for emperors who span the history of humankind. Interestingly, it is quite likely that Marcus himself would have liked to be remembered as a philosopher first, and emperor second.

Chapter Six:

Timeless Lessons from Marcus Aurelius

Learning the histories of people has multiple benefits. Perhaps, two of the most significant benefits are:

- To learn what they did well so that we may emulate their principles in an attempt to achieve success ourselves.

- To learn from their mistakes so that we may avoid similar pitfalls that we could encounter.

Looking at the history of Marcus Aurelius from the above perspective, there are numerous lessons we could learn from the legacy of Meditations as well as the way he led his life. This chapter is dedicated to the timeless lessons that Marcus Aurelius left behind for the benefit of humankind.

Managing rudeness - One of the most important and popular maxims in Meditations is about managing rude people. His advice to manage rudeness goes something like this.

"When you wake up each morning, tell yourself that the people you will meet today will be arrogant, meddling, ungrateful, dishonest, and maybe other negative things. They are that way because they haven't yet understood the true concept of good and evil. However, I learned to see and appreciate the natural beauty of both good and evil and their connection with nature."

"I understand that even though we are not connected through blood, we are connected through the divine or logos. We are all born to do our work, and to feel anger and resentment towards another human being is unnatural. Knowing this makes me immune to the badness and ugliness that such rudeness spreads."

This entry in his journal reflects the fact that Marcus knows he will encounter irksome people right through the day. He is preparing himself to deal with them compassionately and in accordance with Stoic principles.

In the same way, we can learn to prepare ourselves to handle such people in our daily lives. We can do so by controlling our minds and our responses to such people ensuring we don't act and behave in a vengeful way because hate begets hate. Moreover, when we choose to control our minds and emotions regardless of other people's behavior, we are in control of our lives and not the other person, a vital principle of Stoicism.

Living by our choices - Another highly useful lesson we learn from Marcus Aurelius and his Stoic principles is living our lives based on our choices. One quote reads like this, "Choose not to be harmed, and you will not be harmed. If you don't feel the harm, then you are not harmed."

The lesson in this quote is that the choices we make are what drives our lives. If we choose not to feel insulted or slighted or hurt by other people's remarks, we will not feel the pain that usually accompanies hurtful remarks. This lesson is Stoicism is very powerful. To a Stoic, nothing outside of his or her mind and reasoned choices have any value.

Therefore, Marcus teaches us to value what we think of ourselves over what others think of us. If you live by this diktat, then even if someone disagrees with your ideas, you will not feel slighted or hurt because your opinion matters more to you than that of the person who disagrees with you.

Battling unkindness with kindness - Marcus refers to kindness as being an antidote to unkindness. He argues that the proliferation of both these behavioral attitudes depends on how much they are put to use. The more kindness you use, the more kindness will spread and cover a larger section of people who come in contact with you. The same goes for unkindness too.

Therefore, the best way to counter the strength and power of unkindness through kindness. When these opposing elements meet each other, the influence of unkindness will reduce drastically. Moreover, an unkind person is highly likely to return kindness with kindness because they are not prepared to handle kindness. So they simply mimic your kind behavior. Thus, the power of kindness and compassion will increase.

Accepting that negativity, including rude, cruel people, difficult circumstances, and all other forms of negativity, will exist. You cannot do away with these elements of life because that is part of nature. Knowing and accepting this irrefutable truth will help you manage negativity with your positivity.

Therefore, don't be surprised at such people. Instead, expect them and their behaviors and be prepared to handle them with compassion and kindness. Expecting that you will encounter toxic people will help you reduce your feelings of bitterness towards them, which, in turn, helps you present an amiable reaction to their bitterness. Now, the other person is not expecting to meet bitterness with niceness. So, he is likely to feel flabbergasted, and unwittingly, return your favor by reducing his bitterness and negativity.

The trick to remember is that not everyone you meet is going to be a negative person. There are as many positive people and circumstances who will, perhaps, handle your negativity. This lesson is to remind yourself that negativity exists, and you have to be prepared to handle it.

Harming and doing injustice to others is the same as hurting yourself - Hurtful and negative actions degrade us and our personality. When we respect ourselves, we can easily respect others.

Self-respect is inextricably connected with respect for other people. Actions and behaviors that humiliate others end up humiliating ourselves as well.

Marcus further says that self-respect is the only form of respect that really matters in this world. However, most of us don't value it and choose to give it away in exchange for money, fame, or other such materialistic benefits.

The lesson that Marcus teaches us through the acceptance of self-respect is that when we develop the attitude of respecting ourselves, we automatically learn to respect others. Therefore, self-respect teaches us not to take the suffering of other people lightly because their suffering becomes our suffering, and such an attitude reflects our own stained character.

Existing for one another is the nature of human beings - All human beings are destined to exist for one another. We can either endure each other or hate each other. But we cannot escape each other. Each of us is trapped in the net of existence, and we cannot escape from it until death. This knowledge helps us feel compassionate towards one another.

Every person in this world feels pain and loss before he or she dies. Facing this truth strengthens our resolve to live a meaningful and happy life trying to help other human beings instead of living in the misery of hatred, anger, and resentment.

Living life out rightly and truthfully is the only worthy pursuit for human beings - Leading a perfectly righteous life is by itself very, very difficult. Typically, a Stoic ends up using all their time and energy in the pursuit of such a life. Therefore, a true Stoic will never have the time to see what and how others are leading their lives. Even if they do find others who don't follow this maxim, they treat such people with patience and kindness.

Marcus teaches us that other people's choices are their own, and if we learn to respect these choices, then this impatient attitude of ours is a reflection of our own character. He teaches us that if we find people who don't conform to moral expectations, then we must treat instances as opportunities to practice and showcase our patience, and learn to respect such people, regardless of their choices.

When you accept the fact that every human being is flawed, then you can focus your time and energy on what that really matters to you, your own informed, reasoned choices.

Trying to overcome our own faults is far more productive and useful than trying to correct other people's faults. It is foolhardy to try and change everyone around you to align themselves with your needs and expectations. It is impossible and a wasteful effort to try and make everyone so righteous and morally upright that you can make an ideal world for yourself. This effort will only drive you insane.

Instead, it is better to focus on our own faults and make efforts to correct them. In fact, a Stoic feels highly driven to critically examine their personal biases and weaknesses and make all efforts to eliminate, or at least, reduce their interference while making impressions. Examining our own faults and correcting them might take a lifetime. But, it will be a worthy pursuit to follow, considering that with each correction, we will become people than before.

Doing good for its own sake and not for the applause of others - "People who work for fame, especially posthumous fame, forget that the people who remember them will also die soon." This quote from Meditations is like a punch in the face to people who go to any lengths to earn a reputation they believe should last, even after their deaths.

This lesson of Marcus teaches us that regardless of whether someone earns his keep by mowing people's lawns or by earning billions through other means, death is a great equalizer for both these people. Death being a radical equalizer, is the ultimate lesson in humility.

Therefore, we must learn to do good work for its own sake and not for a reputation or to leave behind legacies. Those things, if fated by nature, will happen without your efforts, which should be focused only on doing good and controlling your mind.

He urges us not to focus on external things to make internal changes because nothing can change your internal being except your intention to do so, followed by hard work and commitment. Marcus says, "If you want to build an empire, rule over yourself!"

Learning to accept that endless time will swallow us and everything about us - One particular entry by Marcus in his Meditations goes something like this, "Are you worried about your reputation? Well, we only need to look back in history to know how quickly and easily the abyss of time swallows everything, including the applauding hands into its bottomless pit. Nothing but emptiness remains."

This quote is a stark reminder of our own deaths and its effects on the people who will live after us. When we die, nothing but emptiness will remain, and all our achievements and accolades will slip into nothingness.

The question arises such a scenario - does it make sense to work hard to achieve something? Can it not be better for us to do nothing but simply wait for death whiling away our days, enjoying our time? Marcus' answer to this question is, "The very reason for something to be beautiful and attractive is its impermanence. An ephemeral thing does not lose its beauty because of its fleeting nature. On the contrary, the impermanence renders that thing more beautiful and attractive than if it was permanent."

Therefore, it is our duty to do good work and leave a legacy of goodness for others to follow. You can follow your dreams passionately without worrying about what others think of you and your life.

Knowing all experiences have already been felt by people before us and will be felt by people after us. Again death is the only inevitable thing that is reiterated in the following quote by Marcus, "Bear in mind that the frustrations and pain that we experience have already been experienced by people before us and they have met with death."

In the same way, our frustrations, anger, and pains will disappear into nothingness after our deaths, and new people will experience the same feelings. The only worthy thing to follow is to rigidly examine our feelings and thoughts before giving our approval and assent to the impressions formed in our minds.

This lesson is also useful when we feel overwhelmed by our failures and disappointments. None of us really equip ourselves with the true knowledge of how much we 'need.' We are always looking for that 'little bit more,' which is never satiated. If we focus on our lives, we will see that we were absolutely fine when we had little. But, we wanted more, and then the race of greed started, and it never really reached its completion stage.

Marcus warns us that all of us have enough for our needs. But, nothing can satisfy our greed.

Learning to handle negative emotions - Marcus says, "No place is more peaceful than your own soul. It is a place without disturbances and interruptions. During times of turmoil, retreat into your soul, listen to its advice, gather strength from it, and then return to face your challenges."

In Stoicism, the soul is called the "inner citadel." The inner citadel is the place where there is nothing to do and nothing to achieve. It is a place of total peace and calmness. And the best thing is, it is the place where answers to our questions can be found, if only we had the patience and commitment to looking there for those answers.

Our minds are like the peaceful depths of a deep lake. Regardless of the turmoil and ripples on the lake, the deep part is always still and calm. Our mind is also like the peaceful inner sanctum of a temple whose calmness cannot be disturbed by the bustle and noise in the external parts of the temple.

This inner citadel is the place that will have answers to all your questions. It will also help you manage all the negative emotions in your life if you simply choose to retreat into it. Marcus urges us to retreat into our souls, seek and discover answers to our problems, and then emerge again to handle the challenges of our lives.

Knowing and accepting that a world without pain is impossible - Marcus urges us to ask ourselves, "Is it possible to have a world without pain? Then, how can we ask for the impossible?"

A life without pain may not really be worth living considering that the only way you could possibly have this kind of life is by saying, doing, and being nothing. When we realize that a painless life is impossible, then we can get down to working with our lives so that we can make it as practically happy as possible, embracing the pain that comes with joy.

Accepting that impossibilities don't exist and then getting down to battle will help you look at the terrain with an open mind, Then, the chances of finding solutions automatically increase. You will find exit points that will help you lead a reverent and satisfying life.

Knowing that death is inevitable, and yet there is nothing to fear about it - Marcus says this about death, "After death, there is no 'us' or 'me' to feel pain or suffer harm."

He says that when we are alive, there is no death. When there is death, we are not alive to feel pain or suffering. Therefore, there is nothing to fear about death because it cannot inflict any harm on us. In fact, Marcus believed that death contained freedom of fear. Therefore, encountering death means you are free of fear and its harmful effects.

He further argues that the fear of death is also based on our thinking process. Like any reasoned choice we make, we can choose not to fear death anymore, and the fear will go away.

Knowing that your life could end right now will help you determine the right thing to do - Marcus was adamant that we should accept the irrefutable fact that we could be gone in an instant. There is no guarantee that we will live to see the next moment. Everything in this universe is ephemeral and fleeting.

Human beings have the power to envision the future. We can project themselves into a future, depending on what we want. Using this power, we should always envision a future that does not include us. And this future is what we should use to decide what to do, say, and how to behave today.

He exhorts us to do everything in our lives passionately as if it is the last thing we will do. He urges us to focus on the present because we cannot undo the past, and the future is uncertain, and may not even exist. Wasting time and energy on things like external materialistic elements that add no value to our soul should be avoided.

Instead, we should focus on ourselves and our minds so that we can rigidly examine everything that we experience and sense and make informed and objective choices in life.

He further says, "Nature invited us into her world, and soon she will show us our way out. Darkness will follow soon. The best way to exit nature is by having a calm and serene mind." This approach is essential because you must know that after death, you will be nothing and nowhere. Therefore, the only power you have is how you handle death and its fear.

Further, he explains the concept of death. What is death? It is nothing but a return to the elements. So, in a way, we continue to be part of the whole cosmos except in a constitution quite different from human beings. Death does not end our components that exist in the universe forever and will not perish. Therefore, death might seem like an end to us. But, we continue to exist.

Identifying yourself with your desires and knowing what you want from your life so that your limited time in this world is not wasted - Life is continually testing our desires, wants, and needs. Through various experiences, life is compelling us to find answers to questions like:

- What are our desires?
- How deeply do we desire what we do?
- How do we think we should live?
- What are our priorities?

The answers to such questions form the essence of our life. Marcus believed deeply in this idea. One of the journal entries that reflect this thought goes something like, "At some point in your life, you must identify yourself with your life, recognize which world you belong to, what kind of power rules your world, and what are your roots. With the answers to these questions, you must find a way to free yourself within the time limit given to you in this world. If you lose out using this time effectively, it will be gone and will not return."

Marcus urged himself (and all of us who are fortunate to read his writings) that our time in this world is running out fast. It is up to each of us to find our purpose and live a righteous, meaningful life so that when we meet with death, our minds are calm and serene.

Finally, knowing that soul takes on the color and identity of our thoughts - Marcus says that we literally become our thoughts. This powerful idea is a great way to drive your mind to think the right kind of thoughts. Marcus says that we must learn to guard our mind and its contents ferociously. We must ruthlessly and aggressively filter out elements that are counterproductive to a righteous and moral life.

This lesson is a result of his direct experience. After all, as an emperor, he must have met numerous people day in and day out. It would have been critically important for him to filter the riff-raff from the genuine ones. It is highly likely that repeating this exercise every day would have made Marcus Aurelius a master at filtering out useful and unproductive matter from his mind as well as time-wasting tasks from his life.

We must learn to do the same. Indulge our time and energy on productive work that enhances the power of our soul and avoid getting trapped in thoughts and tasks that affect our soul negatively.

Marcus Aurelius taught us to look at the infinity of time and space before and after us. The huge spasm of time and space that surrounds us is a lesson in humility and acceptance of our tiny space in this vast, ever-expanding universe. And mind you, the philosopher-king was able to see this powerful truth nearly 2000 years ago!

Conclusion

Marcus Aurelius died in 180 A.D. In 178 A.D., he defeated the Germanic tribes in the Danubian region and retired to Vindobona, the winter quarters of the Roman army stationed there. He remained there until he died in 180 A.D.

The legacy of Marcus Aurelius as philosopher-king lies in one interesting difference between his approach to philosophy and those of the more famous ones like Plato, Aristotle, or even Alexander of Aphrodisias and Sextus Empiricus. The other named philosophers were more concerned about the theory of philosophy and epistemology and argued for and against beliefs and ideas. Indeed, such a way of learning philosophy was what was highly prevalent during ancient times.

Marcus Aurelius, on the other hand, chose to rise above mere theoretical arguments and wanted to lead a life based on his philosophical ideals.

Effectively he brought philosophers from books and stage debates in the normal way of life. For him, philosophy was not just trying to understand the world around him rationally but also to convert that understanding into practical exercises using which the people could lead their lives.

This thought is critical in helping you comprehend and appreciate Marcus' collection of daily thoughts in Meditations. This work of Marcus Aurelius can be seen as his true legacy to the world. These journals are completely stripped of all his achievements, regardless of how big or small they were. The work is nothing but a private journal of an emperor, which he used to urge himself to live the best life he could achieve. It is a lesson in self-actualization.

Meditations can, in no way, be called a philosophical treatise of any note. It is just one man's thoughts and the struggles he encounters to achieve peace with himself and the world around him as he is continuously threatened from all directions. He does not really answer the problem of how to achieve peace amidst the chaos in one's life. He only tries to instill self-discipline and discusses

Stoic principles that are designed to avoid self-pity at all costs.

Meditations is a work that reiterates the Stoic view of life wherein everything in the universe is a natural occurrence, whether it is health/sickness, happiness/sadness, disappointment/satisfaction, and even death. The events and emotions by themselves are natural. What frustrates human beings is our interpretation of the events colored by our value-judgments.

The logos is the element that controls everything in the universe, including the fate of human beings. However, how we choose to respond to anything is entirely in our hands, and this element, if handled wisely and properly, is what helps us achieve peace with ourselves and the external world.

Aurelius believed that the universe has the best intentions for us. It is up to us to interpret our life experiences correctly and take advantage of the universe's best intentions for us. We should embrace what life has in store for us instead of trying to resist them and cling on to our opinions and interpretations based on our value-judgments. This approach is what will help us achieve peace in our lives. This lesson is one of the biggest lessons that any emperor could have left behind as a legacy for humanity. Meditations is a work that needs to be interpreted in this way.

There can be little doubt that Marcus Aurelius was one of the most exemplary leaders of all time. He held the most powerful and highest station in the ancient world for almost two decades. He had access to all the luxuries and convenience that wealth and power could offer him at that time. And yet, he chose a life of simplicity and frugality because he believed not just in mere philosophical theories but in practicing a life that was true to these theories.

Moreover, Marcus Aurelius is a constant reminder to us that "absolute power corrupts absolutely" need not always be true. Despite all the struggles he encountered, and despite the absolute power, he wielded never used it for his personal gain in any way whatsoever. He only ensured that he used his absolute power to guide his Empire and its people through the path of virtue and wisdom.

Marcus, despite all his power and influence, did not have an easy life. In fact, some historians believe that he did not get the good fortune he deserved for all the good work he did. But, he did not waver from his duty and rose to the challenge unfailingly each time. He is one of the most inspiring figures from the history of humankind. Reading about him and his works can drive away your most intense of fatigues and frustration, rejuvenating your body and mind to try harder and succeed.

Ending this book on Marcus Aurelius would be best with some of this most powerful quotes that remain relevant even today:

Objective judgment, unselfish action, and willing acceptance, now at this very moment, regardless of all external events. That's all you need.

The wisdom to systematically and authentically investigate every observation that we make in our lives is the most powerful intelligence we can build for ourselves.

Resources

https://www.britannica.com/biography/
Marcus-Aurelius-Roman-emperor

https://www.britannica.com/biography/
Marcus-Cornelius-Fronto

https://www.britannica.com/place/Germany/
Coexistence-with-Rome-to-ad-350#ref62535

https://www.biography.com/political-figure/
marcus-aurelius https://www.britannica.com/
biography/Marcus-Aurelius-Roman-emperor

https://www.ancient.eu/Marcus_Aurelius/

https://stoicjourney.
org/2016/07/28/a-brief-history-of-stoicism/

https://www.iep.utm.edu/marcus/

https://dailystoic.com/marcus-aurelius/

https://reasonandmeaning.com/2015/03/06/marcus-aurelius-a-brief-summary-of-the-meditations/

https://www.britannica.com/topic/Five-Good-Emperors

https://medium.com/@wearestoicelite/10-powerful-lessons-from-marcus-aurelius-meditations-stoic-philosophy-fdc7c1c5ae51
https://www.intellectualtakeout.org/blog/7-timeless-life-lessons-marcus-aurelius/

https://fs.blog/intellectual-giants/marcus-aurelius/

https://fs.blog/2014/08/marcus-aurelius-debts-and-lessons/

Milton Keynes UK
Ingram Content Group UK Ltd.
UKHW022353221123
433027UK00004B/90